rl®

Real Stories From My Time

Samantha™ **TITANIC**

By Emma Carlson Berne

Illustrated by Kelley McMorris

Scholastic Inc.

Published by Scholastic Inc., *Publishers since 1920.* SCHOLASTIC and associated logos are trademarks and/or registered trademarks of Scholastic Inc. The publisher does not have any control over and does not assume any responsibility for author or third-party websites or their content.

Special thanks to Bill Wormstedt

Photos ©: back cover: ullstein bild/The Granger Collection; viii: Patrick Frilet/age fotostock; 12: The Titanic Collection/age fotostock; 13: Library of Congress; 15 top: The Granger Collection; 15 bottom: Phil Yeomans/REX/Shutterstock; 22: Library of Congress; 25: Popperfoto/Getty Images; 26: Everett Historical/Shutterstock; 27: Ilpo Musto/REX/Shutterstock; 29: UniversalImagesGroup/Getty Images; 30: ullstein bild/The Granger Collection; 31: Wikimedia; 36: The Titanic Collection/age fotostock; 44: Library of Congress; 50: Historia/REX/Shutterstock; 60: Library of Congress; 62: United Archives/The Granger Collection; 70: Library of Congress; 79: Library of Congress; 85: Bettmann/Getty Images; 93: Emory Kristof/Getty Images; 100: British Library/Robana/REX/Shutterstock.

Illustrated by Kelley McMorris
Book design by Suzanne M. LaGasa

Library of Congress Cataloging-in-Publication Number: 2017049569

americangirl.com/service

ISBN 978-1-338-19306-0

10 9 8 7 6 5 4 3 2 1   18 19 20 21 22

Printed in the U.S.A.   23

First printing 2018

For Oscar,
my sunshine-faced little boy—
and my last baby

America's past is filled with all kinds of stories. Stories of courage, adventure, tragedy, and hope. The Real Stories From My Time series pairs American Girl's beloved historical characters with true stories of pivotal events in American history. As you travel back in time to discover America's amazing past, these characters go with you to share their own incredible tales.

CONTENTS

TITANIC
WHITE STAR LINE
The Largest Liner
In The World
SOUTHAMPTON ~ NEW YORK
VIA CHERBOURG & QUEENSTOWN

Chapter 1

What Was *Titanic*?

Titanic was a British cruise ship that set sail on April 10, 1912, from Southampton, England, to New York City. At that time, *Titanic* was the largest—and widely believed to be the safest—ship in the world.

Thousands of passengers boarded the luxury ship to begin a journey. Some were returning home to America after traveling in Europe. Others were starting a new life in a country that held the promise of opportunity. Fifteen-year-old Edith Brown was one of

1

those passengers, and she was excited to travel with her parents on *Titanic*. The Browns were a well-to-do family from South Africa. Edith's father wanted to open a hotel in America. As Edith walked up the gangway with her mother and father, she could see the rows and rows of glittering portholes above her. The enormous ocean liner was brand new and beautiful. Until they reached New York, it would be their home.

As the rest of the passengers boarded the ship, each one carried his or her own story. They knew they were making history by sailing on *Titanic*'s very first voyage across the sea. It was the biggest, grandest, most modern ship ever built. Passengers were told that *Titanic* was unsinkable, and they believed it. But the ship's owners were eager to prove that *Titanic* was faster and better than any other vessel. That ambition put every person on board in terrible danger.

In 1904, Samantha Parkington was a nine-year-old orphan growing up in New York. Her parents had died in a tragic boating accident when she was five, so she was being raised to be a proper young lady by her wealthy and old-fashioned grandmother, Grandmary. When she was ten, Samantha moved in with her uncle Gard and aunt Cornelia. She loved her aunt and uncle, but she always longed for a larger family with sisters and brothers.

As Samantha's family was changing, America—and the world—was changing, too. People were inventing new and improved machines to do things faster and better. Samantha rode through the city streets in

Uncle Gard's brand-new automobile. She sailed across the Atlantic Ocean with Grandmary on the luxury ship *Queen Caroline*. She lived in a home with modern devices, such as a telephone and electric lights.

But not everyone lived a life of luxury. Samantha learned this from her best friend, Nellie O'Malley. Nellie and her two younger sisters, Bridget and Jenny, had come from Ireland with their parents for a better life in America. After their parents died of influenza, Nellie and her sisters lived in an orphanage. Samantha was overjoyed when Uncle Gard and Aunt Cornelia decided to adopt Nellie, Bridget, and Jenny. Now the girls could all live together as sisters to Samantha! When Gard and Cornelia's son, William, was born, Samantha finally had the large family she'd always wanted.

In 1912, when Samantha was a teenager, the world watched as the world's largest ship, *Titanic*, set out to make a trip across the Atlantic Ocean. In the middle of the ocean crossing, tragedy struck. For Samantha, the tragedy was personal, because she had family members on board! For days, Samantha waited for news of their fate, praying that another accident wouldn't tear apart her family.

Although Samantha is a fictional character, her story will help you imagine what it was like to live through the *Titanic* disaster.

Samantha's Story

This morning when I come down to breakfast, I see the front page of the *New York News*. Suddenly, I can't breathe. The headline screams "*TITANIC SINKS!*" My heart freezes. My best friend Nellie, Aunt Cornelia, and little William are on *Titanic*! They're sailing home from Ireland. I try to read the words in the newspaper, but they are a blur. All I can think about is Nellie, William, and Cornelia—are they safe? I know I won't stop worrying until I hear from them.

There's a knock on the door. It's Bridget and Jenny. They're here with me at the New York Academy for Young Ladies, and they've just learned about *Titanic*. We fall into one another's arms and cling together.

We decide to go home to be with Uncle Gard. He needs us—and we need him. Bridget and Jenny hurry back to their rooms to pack a bag. I put a clean dress and a petticoat into my suitcase. Every time the doorbell rings downstairs, I jump and listen, hoping I'll hear the maid's footsteps on the stairs and her soft knock telling me there's a telegram from Cornelia. But there's no word yet.

Nellie was so excited for this journey. She hadn't seen Ireland since she left there so many years ago with her parents and sisters. She couldn't wait to go back and show Cornelia and William the country where she was born. They'd been having a lovely time. Her letters were full of descriptions of the beautiful green hills and giant cliffs with the ocean crashing below. Now they're somewhere in the middle of the ocean. I swallow the lump in my throat when I think about how scared they must have been when the ship went down.

I keep hearing Grandmary's voice in my head. She hadn't approved of the fuss over the great ship *Titanic*. I remember her telling Cornelia, "Faster doesn't always mean better, my dear." I can see her clearly, sitting very straight before the fire with her teacup in her hand, shaking her head. Cornelia sat there, listening respectfully, but giving Nellie and me the tiniest of smiles on the side. We all thought sailing on *Titanic* sounded like a wonderful adventure.

Chapter 2

The Grandest Ship

In 1909, the year that construction began on *Titanic*, America was in love with machines. Technology was speeding forward. Mills were churning out yard after yard of cloth. Steel plants were producing sheets of shining hot metal. Metal was used for constructing many things, including railroads, cars, and buildings. Factories were canning fruit so that people could eat peaches in the wintertime. Six years earlier, the Wright brothers had tested their new flying machine in Kitty Hawk, North Carolina. More and more automobiles were replacing horses and carriages on the streets of New York and other cities. It seemed that there was nothing machines could not do.

J. Bruce Ismay, the head of the White Star Line ship company in Great Britain, wanted to make headlines. So he decided to build three magnificent ocean liners. They would be called *Olympic*, *Titanic*, and *Britannic*, and

J. Bruce Ismay

they would be faster, bigger, and more luxurious than any ships the world had ever seen.

The ships were constructed in Belfast, Ireland. The city was known for its shipbuilding, but no one had seen a vessel as enormous as *Titanic*. She rose piece by piece in the **dry docks** alongside her sister ship, *Olympic*, which was just as big and was being constructed at the same time. The two massive ships, weighing 45,000 tons each, were

Olympic and *Titanic* in the shipyard

the largest moving objects ever made up to that point. They towered over Belfast, and every day, people stopped to admire them and wonder at them.

In the early twentieth century—and for centuries before—if you wanted to travel long-distance between the continents, you had to do it by boat. And for hundreds of years, ocean travel was long, dirty, and miserable. The journey from Europe to North America took a month or more. Passengers, whether rich or poor, spent weeks in cold, cramped conditions, and many got sick.

In the 1860s, shipbuilders began designing better boats for long-distance travel. Shipping companies started competing with one another for passengers. One way to do this was to make their ships safer and more comfortable to sail on. Cabins had windows. There was clean water and cleaner bathroom facilities.

Passengers bought tickets based on the level of service they could pay for. First-class tickets were the most expensive and provided the nicest rooms and food. First-class passengers had access to lounges, libraries, and dining rooms. Second-class tickets offered smaller rooms and fewer comforts. Third-class passengers were usually **immigrants**

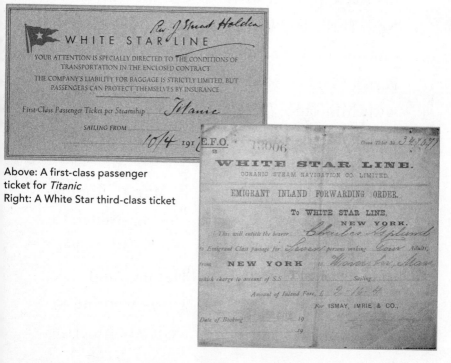

Above: A first-class passenger ticket for *Titanic*
Right: A White Star third-class ticket

or **laborers**. They sailed in cramped quarters on the lowest level of the ship, which was often called **steerage** because it was near the ship's steering machinery.

Robert Douglas Spedden was only six years old when he sailed on *Titanic* in first class. His wealthy family had been traveling in Africa, and now Robert, his parents, and his nurse were headed back to their home in New York. His family's luxury suite in first class had all the comforts the little boy was accustomed to. Robert carried his teddy bear with him onto *Titanic*. He was very excited about the trip, which was the final leg of his family's long journey home.

Although nine-year-old Maria Touma wasn't in first class, she was just as excited to board *Titanic*, clutching a third-class ticket, along with her mother, Hanna, and her younger brother. Her father was working in Michigan, and they were traveling to America to join him there. The Touma family were emigrants from Lebanon. They had already been traveling for weeks by camel, freighter ship, and train. To Maria, even the small room in steerage that she would share with her family during their voyage on *Titanic* felt comfortable by comparison. And it was a relief to know that in just a week they would be in America.

* * *

Improvements to steam engines and propellers made the ships faster. By 1900, it took only about a week to cross from Europe to North America. Shipping companies in Great Britain were major players in the race to build better, faster, and bigger ships. And with *Titanic* and her two sister ships, J. Bruce Ismay was sure he would win this race.

Samantha's Log: Praying for News

Jenny, Bridget, and I are sitting in the library at Gard and Cornelia's house. Uncle Gard is pacing back and forth. No one is talking. The tick of the mantel clock is the only sound in the room. We're all praying for news. The newspaper said most of *Titanic*'s passengers are safe, but I have a terrible feeling in my chest.

I remember when Nellie, Grandmary, her husband Admiral Beemis, and I sailed across the Atlantic on *Queen Caroline* six years ago. She was quite an elegant ship—ships are often referred to as "she" or "her." Although *Queen Caroline* was not as luxurious as *Titanic*, my cozy bed in our first-class cabin had thick curtains around it. When I pulled them closed each night, I stayed toasty warm, despite the cold ocean air.

I had my own little room in our cabin, and my own writing desk. I sat there each day writing in my journal—for fun, I called it my "log." The admiral had told me that ship captains always keep a log, which is a detailed record of the daily happenings of the ship.

I loved to explore the ship. I'll never forget finding my way down to third class. The ship looked different down there. The passengers were crowded and had few of the comforts of the upper decks. Nellie had told me all about traveling in steerage. She and her sisters and parents had traveled that way when they first came to America.

Now, I bow my head and tears drip from my cheeks as Nellie's face swims up in my mind. Will I ever see her again?

Chapter 3

Building a Monstrous Vessel

It took approximately three years and fifteen thousand workers to construct *Titanic* and *Olympic*. The ships were so utterly massive, the shipbuilders had to make new equipment before they could even start to build. The largest **gantry** in the world was put up—228 feet high—to support *Titanic* and *Olympic* while they were being built.

As construction continued, the ships began to soar above the Belfast skyline. The three giant bronze-and-steel propellers were attached. The massive anchors—three per ship—were brought in on specially constructed wagons, each pulled by a team of twenty powerful Shire draft horses. Three million rivets held in place the one-inch-thick steel plates of the **hull**.

Titanic and *Olympic* would move rapidly through the water using steam power to run their state-of-the-art engines. Steam power

Titanic had three propellers—two wing, or outer propellers; each with three blades, and one center propeller with four blades

had been used to power trains and ships for a long time. It was made by shoveling coal into huge boilers. *Titanic* had twenty-nine of them! The boilers would give off the steam, which would pass through the engines. The engines would turn the propellers, moving the ship forward. *Titanic* had three large engines of the newest, fastest kind—they had recently been used in other new ocean liners with great success.

Olympic was finished first. During one of her early voyages, *Olympic* was hit by another ship. Water got into two of the watertight compartments but *Olympic* still made it back to port. So people were reassured. They believed that *Titanic* could not be sunk.

During the building process, *Titanic* was tested in the water. This was standard for all ships. *Titanic* was slid slowly off the slip on which she was built and into the water. Her engines and boilers were loaded in later at the fitting-out dock. *Titanic* was simply a huge floating shell, and she floated beautifully. It was time to outfit *Titanic* on the inside.

The interior of *Titanic* was very fancy so as to impress wealthy passengers. There was a sweeping grand staircase, topped by a beautiful glass dome. A gym had all the latest exercise equipment, like stationary bicycles and rowing machines. There was a swimming pool, something that was not usually found on ships, and an indoor court to play the game of squash.

First-class passengers' rooms were located in the middle of the ship, where the rocking of the boat wouldn't be felt as much as in other places. Some first-class passengers had larger rooms—suites—that had private bathrooms. Some suites even had a private deck. All first-class rooms had telephones, heaters, and special lamps that wouldn't tip over if the ship sailed through choppy waters.

A barbershop and smoking rooms full of

A cabin on the first-class deck on *Titanic*

comfortable leather chairs, provided places for the gentlemen. Elegant lounges and light-filled sitting rooms were available for the ladies. A Reading and Writing Room had tables, soft chairs, and sofas. The library was lined floor to ceiling with leather-bound books for people to borrow and read on board. There were several places to eat on *Titanic*. The first-class dining room was the largest room on the ship. In the Verandah Café or the Café Parisien, ladies could have tea and light snacks in between meals.

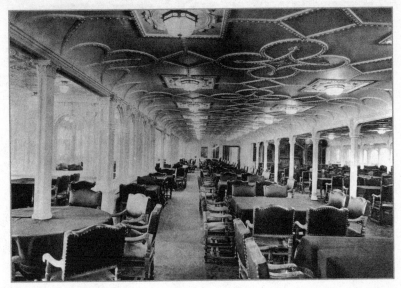
The dining room of *Titanic*

The third-class accommodations on *Titanic* were nicer than most second-class rooms on older ships. In the past, people in steerage— third class—would sleep and eat in one large crowded room, in the lowest part of the ship. There was no place for them to go for fresh air or exercise. They had to use buckets instead of toilets. *Titanic*'s third class was made up of small cabins that included bunk beds, pillows, and blankets. There was running water and electricity. Cabins even had sinks so that passengers could wash up in their own rooms. Third class had its own smoking room, dining room, and lounge. Passengers could walk and stroll on the lower decks and get fresh air.

Although the ship was believed by many to be unsinkable, it was built with all the modern safety measures. She had sixteen watertight compartments to prevent her from ever sinking. If—*if*—water should enter one or two of the compartments—even four—the

A re-creation of a third-class cabin on *Titanic*

ship could still stay afloat. The water would be sealed in and would not penetrate the rest of the ship. White Star made sure there were enough life jackets for every passenger. And there were lifeboats, too—the ship was required to have them. *Titanic* had sixteen wooden lifeboats and four collapsible boats. These boats could hold 1,178 people. But the ship was designed to carry 3,547 passengers and crew. Mr. Ismay, the head of White Star, saw no need for more lifeboats on board. He wasn't breaking any laws—the ship wasn't required to carry any more than they already had. Mr. Ismay didn't want additional life-boats blocking the view of the ocean from the first-class deck. Mr. Ismay didn't worry about the number of lifeboats. He believed that *Titanic* was unsinkable. The lifeboats would never be needed—or so he thought.

* * *

April 10, 1912. The day of *Titanic*'s maiden voyage—her first trip—had arrived. Fresh paint gleamed inside and outside the ship. The beds were made. The forks were polished. In the boiler room, men heaved shovelfuls of coal into the boilers. The great engines were slowly revving up.

The crew stood ready wearing dark blue uniforms, the gold buttons sparkling in the

An inspector examining the lifebelts (lifejackets) on *Titanic*

spring sunshine. Soon after ten o'clock in the morning, passengers began to stream onto the ship. One of the passengers was seven-year-old Eva Hart, who was traveling with her mother, Esther, and her father, Benjamin. The family was on their way to live in Canada, where her father was going to open a drugstore. Eva was excited. Sailing on *Titanic* seemed an excellent way to start their adventures in a foreign land.

Titanic departing on her maiden voyage, April 10, 1912

Eva Hart (center) with her parents

But Eva's mother was not excited—she was scared! Eva remembered many years later, "We went down to the cabin and that's when my mother said to my father that she had made up her mind quite firmly that she would not go to bed in that ship . . . and she didn't!" Eva's mother had a feeling that something would go terribly wrong on the ship.

Samantha's Log: Memories of Setting Sail

No news yet of Cornelia, Nellie, and William. The maid has brought us a tray of sandwiches. Jenny, Bridget, and I have tried to eat, but Gard can't. He just drinks coffee and stares out the window. I've brought some of my schoolbooks in an attempt to distract myself. Inside my geography book, I find the clipping I cut from the paper the day *Titanic* set sail: April 10. Reading again about the magnificent ship steaming out of Southampton, England, makes me think about when we set sail on *Queen Caroline*. We launched at midnight, and I begged Grandmary to let me stay up to watch our departure. The ship was lit with a million white light bulbs, and everybody crowded to the rails and threw flowers in the water and waved to the people on shore.

The newspaper clipping says that *Titanic* set sail at noon. The ship's band played on the deck, and the giant steam whistle blew three times. The tugboats guided the ship out of the harbor while people on the dock cheered and passengers waved from the railings. A lump rises in my throat as I think of Cornelia, Nellie, and William laughing and waving from the deck of *Titanic*. Where are they now?

Chapter 4

A Pleasant Life On Board

The weather was perfect those first days on *Titanic*. The sea was very calm; the sky was blue. Life on board a ship, in the days before television and smartphones, was relaxed. A first-class passenger might start the day with a swim in the six-foot-deep heated saltwater pool. Ladies could sew, read, or write letters in the Reading and Writing Room. Passengers spent a lot of time strolling on the decks, wrapped up in furs and coats against the ocean breeze. When they

Passengers on the deck of *Titanic*

got tired, they could sit on deck chairs and let the **steward** bring them a hot drink. In the late afternoon and at dinnertime, an eight-piece band provided live music.

When it was time for harder exercise, passengers could play squash, a game similar to tennis, in the onboard court for a fee of fifty cents per game. Or they could work out in the gymnasium, where the Scottish instructor, Thomas McCawley, would show them how to use the rowing machine or one of the other modern pieces of gym equipment.

If someone had a message to send to relatives or friends, she could send a telegram via *Titanic's* state-of-the-art communications system. Two **telegraph** operators, Jack Phillips and Harold Bride, would tap out the message in **Morse code**. The first ten words cost about three dollars and twelve cents, and each additional word was about nineteen cents. That was a lot of money in those days, so only wealthy people sent telegrams.

On the second-class passengers' deck, stewards provided deck games such as ring toss and shuffleboard. Board games like chess and backgammon were also played.

Steerage passengers couldn't use the pool or the gym, but they could stroll on part of the lower deck, or read and write in the third-class common room. One man brought his bagpipes and played for everyone. Other passengers most likely brought instruments as well, and there was probably dancing. Children and teenagers played jump rope. A gang of eight boys made a game of climbing onto a baggage crane. They didn't know that it had been greased, though, and promptly fell off!

No one went hungry on *Titanic*—in fact, meals were high points of the day. For dinner in first class, men would wear tuxedos with a white tie, the fanciest kind. Women would dress in elegant evening gowns that would shimmer with sparkling beads or drip with lace. First-class children would dress for dinner, too, the girls in their nicest dresses and hair bows and the boys in little suits. But most of the time, children did not eat with their parents. In first class, ships had earlier dinner hours just for the children, where they would eat with their nannies.

For the adults, first-class dinnertime was six o'clock. Dinner was announced by a bugler marching from deck to deck playing a song called "The Roast Beef of Old England." The tables would be set with white tablecloths, glittering silverware, and crystal wineglasses. Diners would eat their way through a soup course, a fish course, a meat course, then dessert, followed by cheese and coffee. First-class dinners could last three hours. Of course, everyone would use their very best table manners.

Third-class food was much less extravagant than the other classes', but passengers still considered the meals a luxury. It used to be that third-class passengers had to bring their own food on an ocean voyage. But on *Titanic*, meals were provided. Breakfast might be oatmeal with milk, smoked fish, and potatoes with tea or coffee. Dinner could be codfish, rice, and bread and jam. Many steerage passengers considered the food the best they had ever had.

Samantha's Log: Setting Records

As I wait for news of *Titanic*, I've been thinking more about my time on the *Queen Caroline*. One night, we dined at the Captain's Table. It was a great honor to sit there. The other people at the table asked the captain how fast we were going. Later, Admiral Beemis explained to me that some of the men made bets on how fast the ship was moving and when she would reach England. He said that new ships want to set speed records, so they compete against one another.

I hear Grandmary's voice in my head, saying, "Faster isn't always better." And I wonder . . . how fast was *Titanic* going when she struck that iceberg?

Chapter 5

All in the Ship Together

*T*itanic was a very fancy ship—and she had some very fancy passengers. Many of them were both rich and famous, like John Jacob Astor IV. This fabulously wealthy businessman boarded *Titanic* with his young wife, Madeleine. Madeleine was only eighteen (Astor was forty-seven), and she was pregnant with their first child.

Isidor and Ida Straus were on the ship, too. Isidor was a co-owner of Macy's department store. This wealthy couple had been married for over forty years and they were extremely close. They'd been known to write each other letters if they were separated for even one day.

Many of the people in second class and third class were leaving Europe and **emigrating** to the United States or Canada to make a new and better life there. One second-class passenger, a French man named Michel Navratil, was fleeing France. He had

Isidor Straus

kidnapped his young sons from their mother. Michel Jr. and Edmond were only three and two when their father boarded *Titanic* under the false name Hoffman.

Anna Sofia Sjöblom was leaving her home as well. She was traveling third class from Finland to visit her father, who was working in the forests of Olympia, Washington. But Anna wasn't even supposed to be on *Titanic*. She and three friends had actually bought tickets for another ship, *Adriatic*. But there was a coal shortage and *Adriatic* couldn't sail. Anna and her friends were relieved and excited to be transferred to the famous *Titanic*. But when the ship began moving, some of Anna's excitement wore off. Her stomach rolled constantly with seasickness. She barely moved from her bed—even on April 14, her eighteenth birthday.

Eva Hart was traveling in second class and was having a much better time than

Anna. *Her* stomach felt just fine, and she spent as much time as she could exploring the ship. She fell in love with a little dog who was traveling on board and rushed through her breakfast every morning so she could play with him. Eva's father had given her a large teddy bear when they were in London. Eva let her playmate, a six-year-old named Nina Harper, play with the bear, too. Everyone in second class smiled at the two little girls dragging the big teddy bear all over the ship with them.

Eight-year-old Marjorie Collyer was traveling with her mother and father in third class. The family was going to emigrate from their home in Hampshire, England, to Idaho. Mrs. Collyer had **tuberculosis**, which affected many people in those days, and the Collyers thought the Idaho climate would be good for her health. The Collyers emptied their bank account and brought all the money they had in the world with them on *Titanic*. They were full of hope and headed for a new life. Their church in England had given them a beautiful send-off with a bell-ringing concert. Their friends surrounded them, saying good-bye, offering hugs and handshakes. *Write to us from America,* they urged. And the Collyers promised they would.

Titanic was also full of workers. Over nine hundred crew members kept the ship running. This included the sailors who operated the ship and the stewards who waited on the passengers. The engineers and firemen kept the tremendous engines and boilers running, and the masters-at-arms acted as the ship's policemen. There were cooks, waiters, bellboys, pot scrubbers, laundry workers, cleaning staff, musicians, postal clerks, a butcher, and even elevator operators. Two fourteen-year-old boys were the youngest crew members. Frederick Hopkins was a plates steward—he would clear and wash plates after meals. William Watson was a bellboy—he would run errands for the passengers. Almost all the crew was from England. For most of them, this voyage would be their last.

Captain E. J. Smith was in charge of the ship and the crew. This veteran ship's captain had commanded White Star Line's ships since 1897 and became commodore, a naval officer higher in rank than captain, of White Star in 1904 and had sailed two million miles total! Now he was ready to take the wheel for the last time before he retired—*Titanic*'s very first voyage. Captain Smith was the ideal man for the job—he was well known, and wealthy passengers loved him. He knew how to guide giant ships through dangerous situations. In fact, Smith demonstrated his skill when *Titanic* almost collided with another ship, *New York*, just as she was pulling out of Southampton Harbor. *Titanic* was so powerful that when she started to move, the ropes that tied *New York* to the dock were sucked under *Titanic*. *New York* drifted toward *Titanic* and for a moment, the crew thought the two ships would hit each other. But Captain Smith knew what to do. He ordered the port—the left—engine fired up just a little more. This bit of power pushed *New York* away from *Titanic* just enough to avoid an accident. Smith's experience and skill had spared the ship—it seemed like a good omen.

First Officer William Murdoch had seen Captain Smith's skill at guiding ships first-hand. Before sailing on *Titanic*, Murdoch had worked on *Titanic*'s sister ship, *Olympic*, under Captain Smith. Murdoch was to assist Captain Smith at steering and navigating the ship. Murdoch was from Scotland and came from a long line of sea captains and sailors. He himself had gone to sea when he was only thirteen and was more comfortable on the deck of a ship than on land.

Murdoch and the other officers spent most of their time on the upper front deck of the ship—called the bridge—and the wheelhouse, which faced the sea. But other crew members barely saw the sky and water. Down in the **bowels** of the ship, firemen—or stokers, as they were called—shoveled giant

Captain E. J. Smith

amounts of coal into the furnaces, to fire the boilers that kept the ship running. The boiler rooms could get as hot as 120 degrees Fahrenheit. The firemen often worked only in their undershirts and shorts due to the extreme heat. It was also very dirty and sooty down in the boiler rooms—the firemen were called the "black gang," because their skin became black from coal dust and smoke. Frederick Barrett was one of the lead stokers on *Titanic*. He was twenty-eight and was from Liverpool, England. Frederick had worked on ships before. He was used to the hard work of shoveling coal all day.

Titanic was like a floating town with people from all parts of society on board. Just by boarding the ship, the passengers and the crew were linked together. Their fates were intertwined—for better or worse.

Samantha's Log: Hoping for a Better Life

The newspaper is full of stories of the people aboard *Titanic*. The paper says that many of the second- and third-class passengers were from Ireland. I can see the pain in Bridget and Jenny's eyes as they read this. When they originally arrived in America, many people thought that Nellie and her sisters were dirty and had diseases, just because they were from Ireland. In the city, I discovered that many immigrants live in cold, crowded rooms in run-down buildings because that's all they can afford. Children don't always go to school— many have to work. Grown-ups have a hard time finding work because people don't want to hire some- one from another country. Before I met Nellie, I didn't see the **prejudice** all around me. Nellie opened my eyes to the truth about how immigrants and poor people are often treated by the wealthy, and I've never forgotten the lessons she taught me.

Chapter 6

Iceberg!

Titanic had been at sea for four days. The weather had been perfect. And the night of April 14 was no exception. The sea was very calm—in fact, it was the flattest water Second Officer Lightoller, the officer on watch, could ever remember. The black water of the North Atlantic stretched out endlessly until it met the spectacular star-dusted sky.

The night was very cold. The North Atlantic was always cold in April, but that night the temperature dropped to just above

55

freezing. The ship was steaming forward, and it was going fast. Captain Smith had been increasing the speed of the ship each day. This was normal practice for a first voyage. Now, the giant ship was plowing through the darkness at a rate of twenty-two-and-a-half knots, which is the equivalent of a car driving twenty-five miles an hour. *Titanic* was almost at a top speed of twenty-three knots. Since they didn't have to worry about traffic, ships often operated at full speed, even at night.

Beep-beep-be-be-beep. Senior Operator Jack Phillips hunched over his telegraph machine, listening through his headphones. He scrawled the incoming messages on slips of paper. Four other steamships in the area had telegraphed ice warnings that day to *Titanic*, saying that they had spotted icebergs in the area and to watch out. Icebergs were common in that part of the sea, at that time of the year. The crew knew that icebergs could break open the hull of a ship, even a steel hull like *Titanic*'s. And a ship as big as *Titanic* could not swerve or turn quickly. Still, no one really thought the mighty ship was in danger, because she was so big and powerful.

Phillips delivered the warnings to the bridge so that the captain and crew would see them. Then the captain could decide whether to slow down, or change course. But Phillips was very busy—besides the ice warnings, he had a pile of personal messages from the passengers to transmit that night. So when he received one last message that night from the ship *Mesaba* about a tremendous ice field directly in *Titanic*'s path, he merely replied, "Received, thanks." And that was all. Phillips never delivered the message to the bridge. The captain and the crew never saw it.

Meanwhile, on the bridge, Captain Smith and Second Officer Lightoller were aware of the ice situation. They had seen the warnings and they knew this part of the ocean well. Because of the ship's speed, they knew they must keep an eye out for the ice—a collision with an iceberg could damage the ship or slow her down. So the captain and second officer agreed that if visibility became reduced, they would slow down.

Perched high up above the ship in the lookouts' nest, sailors Archie Jewell and George Symons were doing their job, peering through the dark, looking for ice. If they saw any, they were to use the telephone to call down to the bridge and sound an alarm. Jewell and Symons were watching for a ring of white foam that formed at the bottom of icebergs when the waves crashed against them. Most of an iceberg is hidden under-water, so this was the best way to spot one in the dark. But there were no waves that night—the sea was glassy calm. And Jewell and Symons had another problem—they had no binoculars. No one could find them. Yet the lookouts weren't terribly worried. Everyone on the crew believed that nothing truly bad could happen to *Titanic*.

Elsewhere on the ship, the evening musical concerts ended. The air had become much colder. A few men sat awake, talking over drinks and cigars in the smoking room, and a young couple from Michigan on their honeymoon, Dickinson and Helen Bishop, shivered in the lounge. Most passengers wandered back to their rooms and got ready for bed. A young man named Lawrence Beesley lay reading in his bunk. He noticed the boat vibrating more than usual from the increased speed. Beesley didn't know why exactly, but he'd an urge to get his life jacket down from the wardrobe in his room earlier that evening.

By 10:00 p.m., the off-duty crew members went to bed. Captain Smith went to his cabin.

Officer Lightoller went to bed. Lookouts Frederick Fleet and Reginald Lee took over for Jewell and Symons. By 11:00 p.m., the ship was dark and quiet. The powerful engines hummed and the giant propellers churned in the frigid black waters.

Operator Jack Phillips was still hard at work transmitting personal messages from the passengers. One more ice warning came in. This time, the message was from the nearby ship *Californian*. "Say, old man,"

Frederick Fleet

the message read. "We are stopped and surrounded by ice." "Shut up! Shut up! I am busy," Phillips replied. That was the last communication between the two ships. The *Californian* operator shut his telegraph down and went to bed.

Up on deck, First Officer Murdoch was on duty. The temperature outside had dropped below freezing, and the cold air pierced through his woolen officer's coat. He had to move to keep warm. Murdoch paced about, keeping an eye on the water and on the crew.

It was 11:39 p.m. The ship steamed ahead. She was going tremendously fast. The lookouts watched the sea. Fleet saw it first: a black hulking thing directly in their path. He picked up the telephone. "Iceberg right ahead!" he shouted.

Murdoch hollered to **Quartermaster** Hichens, who was manning the wheel, to turn the rudder hard to the right. Then Murdoch

Icebergs are huge, with most of the sharp ice hidden below the water

telegraphed to the engine room to stop. He needed to turn *Titanic* out of the iceberg's path. Could the giant ship respond in time?

On the bridge, the crew waited. For nearly a minute they watched, tense and anxious. Would the ship turn in time? Slowly, slowly, the nose of the ship eased over to the left. They had avoided a head-on collision! The crew members sighed with relief.

Suddenly, a tremendous scraping noise, a groaning of metal against ice, reverberated through the ship. In the first-class smoking

room, men leapt to their feet as the ship rat-
tled and shuddered. A woman trying to sleep
in her bunk later recalled hearing a noise like
rocks tumbling together. A second-class passenger who was reading the newspaper in her
bunk said later that it sounded like ice skates
scraping on ice.

Titanic had avoided a head-on strike, but
it had still run into the iceberg. The sharp ice
sliced through the side of the ship. The hull
had been damaged, but just how badly, no
one yet knew.

Chapter 7

Horror at Sea

Captain Smith, who was in his cabin, raced onto the bridge a moment after the ship struck the iceberg. Murdoch quickly told him what had happened. Captain Smith and the ship's designer, Thomas Andrews, rushed down to the lower levels to look at the damage. They stared in horror. The iceberg had punched deep gashes in the ship's steel-plated hull over an area about three hundred feet long. Icy water was rushing into the ship's watertight compartments. There was no way to seal the holes and stop the water, and it was coming in faster than it could be pumped out.

Smith and Andrews knew the unthinkable was about to happen. The ship was going to sink.

An hour and a half. That's how much time Andrews estimated the ship had before she was underwater. The passengers had to get off the ship—and fast. Smith swung into action. He sent a message to the telegraph room to put out a distress call. *Titanic* needed help. Another ship must come to her rescue. It was the only hope for the 2,208 people on board.

The stewards told passengers to report to the decks with their life jackets on. Few people seemed worried. Many thought it was just a precaution and that they'd be allowed to go back to their rooms shortly. The ship's band played lively tunes as passengers waited for instruction. But those who were below deck began to notice strange things. Third-class passenger Carl Jonsson was dressing in his room, preparing to go up to the deck as instructed, when he saw water creeping under his door.

Just after midnight, Captain Smith ordered the lifeboats launched. People were calm and quiet as they filed on deck. First-class passengers stood with their white life jackets strapped around fur coats. The first lifeboats were slowly lowered down the side of the enormous ship. But they were only half-full. The crew was worried that the lifeboats might crack or buckle under the weight of all the people as they were lowered down to the sea. Many people did not want to get into the boats. The sea was cold and dark, and the ship didn't *seem* to be sinking. They still believed that *Titanic* would not sink—or that if she did, they would surely be rescued by another ship. Perhaps that's why the crew launched the first lifeboats only half-filled.

In the telegraph room, Operator Phillips sent out distress calls for help—over and over. The ship *Carpathia* said she was on her way, coming as fast as she could. How far away? Captain Smith asked. Fifty-eight miles, Phillips told him. This was bad news and Captain Smith knew it. *Carpathia* would take four hours to reach them. *Titanic* would not stay afloat that long. There were not enough lifeboats for everyone—not nearly enough. Captain Smith knew that a lot of people were going to die. He knew that he would be one of them. As captain, it was his job to stay with his ship, no matter what.

Fffoom! The quartermaster began firing distress rockets into the sky every five minutes. He hoped a nearby ship might see them and come to help. The rockets finally jolted the passengers into believing that the disaster was real. Some began to pray. Some panicked. The crew began to restrict the lifeboats to women and children only. Men were no longer allowed. Families were separated as husbands and fathers loaded wives, daughters, and sons onto the boats.

Marjorie Collyer clung to her father, Harvey. Her mother, Charlotte, hung on to both. A crew member tore Marjorie from her father's arms and nearly threw her into one of the boats. They pulled Marjorie's mother in behind her. Harvey stood calmly on the deck, watching, as the boat with his family was lowered into the sea. It was the last time Marjorie and Charlotte would see him.

Ida Straus refused to be separated from her husband. "We have been living together for many years," she told Isidor when he tried to put her in a lifeboat. "And where you go, I go." That was that. The couple sat down in deck chairs and waited together.

Charlotte Collyer with her daughter, Marjorie, after the sinking of *Titanic*

John Jacob Astor helped his young, pregnant wife into a lifeboat. He quietly asked if he might get in as well. He was refused and stepped away. Madeleine and her unborn baby survived. Astor did not.

Samantha's Log: Tragedy in the Water

This morning, April 17, the headline in the *New York News* is staring me in the face: "Only 868 Alive of 2,200 on Sunken Liner *Titanic*. Death Toll of 1,300. No Hope Left of Any Boatloads Being Picked Up." My mouth goes dry as I stare down helplessly at the paper, not wanting to believe it. Bridget and Jenny aren't down to breakfast yet and I'm glad. I don't want them to see this—just for a few more minutes. Then a hand reaches out and covers my own. I look up into Uncle Gard's face. His eyes are filled with tears and my heart aches. He clears his throat. "I haven't forgotten your parents, you know, Sam," he says gently. My father and mother—she was Uncle Gard's sister—both died in a boating accident when I was five. It was a terrible time for our whole family. I try to speak but choke and squeeze his hand instead. I know we have to be strong for Bridget and Jenny—and for each other.

Chapter 8

Desperate to Survive

Passengers began rushing the lifeboats, scrambling to save themselves. Captain Smith and some officers opened the weapons cabinet. An officer fired above the crowd to keep men from trying to board the boats while women were still on deck. A huge man jumped into a lifeboat as it was being lowered and knocked a woman unconscious. One lifeboat was almost lowered on top of another. Only quick thinking by crew members saved the people in the lower boat from being crushed.

Down in steerage, Anna Sjöblom and her three friends ran through the maze of hallways and passages, determined to get to the lifeboats. They stumbled toward a doorway leading to the upper decks, then stopped, staring at one another in horror. Metal grates had been pulled across the doorway openings and locked. The crew was keeping steerage passengers from getting to the lifeboats! Anna and her friends—everyone in third class— were trapped. Anna made up her mind that she was not going to be drowned. She found a hard object and smashed a window. She climbed out into the frigid ocean air and up and over the outside of the ship to the upper decks. Anna made it into a lifeboat. Her friends did not.

Maria Touma loved playing in the vacant cabins on the ship. On the night of the sinking, her mother looked everywhere for her and couldn't find her. She brought Maria's brother to the boat deck and returned to search frantically for Maria. She finally found her asleep in a vacant third-class cabin. Maria, her mother, and her brother boarded a lifeboat and were lowered off *Titanic*.

The two young Navratil boys, whose father had kidnapped them, were wrapped in blankets and given to a woman in a lifeboat. Michel and Edmond's father never made it off the ship. The toddlers were the only children without guardians who survived.

As the huge ship filled with water, she began leaning to the left. The front part, the **bow**, was starting to tilt underwater. At 1:15 a.m., the bow went under. Even though the ship was partially submerged, the lights still blazed brightly. To some passengers in the lifeboats, it still seemed unimaginable that the "unsinkable" ship was going underwater.

On the upper deck, the band continued to play cheerily. Some people were having drinks in the smoking room. Some passengers were even working out on the gym equipment, helped by the instructor. They may have been in shock. They may have accepted that they were going to die. Or perhaps they still didn't believe that the ship was sinking, even though part of it was now underwater.

As the bow of the ship slid farther under the water, the last lifeboats were loaded.

Down in the bowels of the ship, the firemen were risking their lives to keep the boilers going so that the ship's lights and telegraph system could keep working. Operators Phillips and Bride stayed at their posts, transmitting distress messages. At 2:05 a.m., Captain Smith told them to leave their posts and save themselves.

Fifteen hundred people were still on board. One group huddled in a great circle, praying. Some jumped off the side of the ship. At 2:10

a.m., the bow of the ship was underwater, and the **stern**, or the back of the ship, tilted sharply upward. From the lifeboats out on the ocean, survivors watched the surreal sight of the brilliantly lit ship rising up into the air. The masses of people on board scrambled desperately toward the high end of the ship, but it was steeply tilted. Crossing to the other end of the deck was like climbing up a slippery slide. People tried to hold on by clinging to deck rails or ropes, but many fell, screaming, into the sea.

The stern rose higher into the air. The band played one last tune. Then, seven minutes later, at 2:17 a.m., the stern of the ship rose straight up out of the water, exposing the huge propellers. *Titanic*'s bow had filled with water and was going down. Survivors remember a massive screeching, crashing groan as everything in the ship, from china cups to grand pianos, slid down from one end of the ship to the other. *Titanic*'s lights went out. Now the whole forward half of the ship was completely underwater. The ship was breaking apart, into two pieces. The stern was still upright, almost vertical, above the water. As the ship broke apart, the stern slowly settled back into the water. It floated for a few seconds, then rose up straight in the water, bobbing like a cork. Survivors remember the stern floating upright for anywhere from thirty seconds to three minutes. The last few passengers clinging to the ship were screaming and wailing. Then the stern slipped underwater. *Titanic* was gone.

Hundreds of people had fallen into the water, and they were struggling to stay alive. They were wearing life jackets, so most of them did not die from drowning. They froze to death in the icy waters, screaming, moaning, and begging for help. Passengers in the lifeboats floated just out of reach. Some of the lifeboats were only half-filled and had room for more survivors, but the people in the lifeboats didn't go back.

They were afraid that the people in the water would overload the small boats and **capsize** them. As they waited for a ship to rescue them, the survivors listened to the sounds of people dying all around them. Gradually,

Titanic survivors on lifeboats

the sounds faded away, replaced only with silence. Those in the water were dead.

In the end, only one crew member took a lifeboat and went back into the mass of dead to look for survivors. With his flashlight piercing the black night, Fifth Officer Lowe searched through the frozen bodies. He found only four people alive. One man died just after he was pulled into the lifeboat.

Samantha's Log: Still Waiting

This morning, the newspaper headlines said that only 705 survivors were on board. The paper is full of articles about the survivors, many of whom are rich and famous. We care nothing for the rich and famous in this house—we think only of our beloved Nellie, Cornelia, and William! Uncle Gard is trying to stay hopeful for me and the girls. Bridget and Jenny are, too. "Maybe they're on the *Carpathia*, wrapped in blankets," Bridget said at breakfast. "Maybe they're sipping hot tea right now," I chimed in. Then we couldn't keep it up anymore. The silence surrounded us once more. Jenny began to cry, her sobs the only sound in the room.

Chapter 9

After the Disaster

Rescue arrived at dawn—for those who were left to receive it. The ship *Carpathia* steamed into view. Survivors—wet, frozen, **hypothermic**, and traumatized—were hauled on board in slings, in bags, and up rope ladders. They were treated as kindly as possible—given warm blankets, dry clothes, hot food and coffee, and as much medical attention as the ship could offer. The deck was crowded with bundled-up survivors sitting numbly in deck chairs, still stunned, or wandering around, looking for family who were not there.

Carpathia, which had been headed for Europe, set a new course for New York. The three-day journey was slow and sad, with many icebergs and rough seas. The news was broadcast over the telegraph wires. "A World Waiting" read one newspaper headline on April 18.

Newspapers wrote of the *Titanic* disaster daily and in great detail, partly because of the high number of famous and wealthy people on board. The US government, and later the British government, held an **inquiry** into the disaster. Charities were set up so people could donate money for the survivors. For weeks after the sinking, many of the bodies of the dead, still floating in their life jackets, were pulled from the ocean's surface and buried. As for the survivors, they tried to put their lives back together again.

Robert Douglas Spedden was alive. He had made it into a lifeboat along with both his parents and his nurse. Wrapped in a blanket, Robert slept all through the sinking of the ship, waking only at dawn. He told his nurse that they were at the North Pole, but there was no Santa Claus to be seen.

Front page of *The Chicago Daily Tribune* for Tuesday, April 16, 1912

Edith Brown had made it off *Titanic* as well. Her father had put her and her mother into a lifeboat, then stood on the deck, smoking a cigar and sipping a glass of brandy as the lifeboat was lowered down the side of the sinking ship. All through that long, cold night, Edith listened to the screams of the freezing, dying people in the water. It was a sound she was never to forget for the rest of her life.

No one knew how to identify the two kidnapped toddlers, Michel and Edmond Navratil. Their father had given a fake name to the ship company, and now he was dead. But Michel and Edmond's mother recognized her babies from their picture in the newspaper. She sailed to America and was reunited with her sons in New York. They returned to France soon after, where the boys grew up. Anna Sjöblom married an American and had a family. Sadly, Charlotte

Collyer and little Marjorie returned to England, where Charlotte died two years later, leaving Marjorie an orphan. Madeleine Astor remained in New York and had her baby. Her son, John Jacob VI, inherited some of his family's fortune. But he grew up never knowing his father.

Samantha's Story Continues

There's a knock at the front door. I bolt up in my chair, my heart hammering, as the maid opens the library door. "Telegram, sir." She hands Uncle Gard a small yellow envelope. He fumbles with the flap. His face is white. We press in around him. I can hardly bear to look at the typed words—yet I can't bear not to. "We are all safe on Carpathia. To dock at New York harbor 3:00 p.m. Love Cornelia."

They're safe, they're all safe! Tears stream down my cheeks as I grab Jenny and Bridget in my arms. Uncle Gard kisses the telegram and presses it against his chest. "Thank God, thank God!" is all we can say. The pressure that has built inside me for the last five days releases as if someone has opened up a valve in my heart, and I sob with relief.

We quickly dress to go meet the ship at the dock. With trembling hands, I pin on my hat and wrap my shawl around my shoulders. Out on the street, we dodge automobiles and coal wagons as we walk swiftly toward the docks. As we draw nearer, more and more people seem to be heading in the same direction. Then I see her—the massive steamship pulled up at harbor. CARPATHIA, read the big white letters on the side of her hull.

"Look!" Jenny points. As the crew lowers the **gangplank**, we can see the survivors, wrapped in blankets and shawls, crowding the ship's railings and then streaming down the gangplank to the docks. People are waving and crying out as they see their loved ones. Where are Nellie and Cornelia? Where is William? Why aren't they here? Silently we scan the ship, Bridget and Jenny standing on their tiptoes. Has something happened during the last hours of the journey?

Then—"Samantha!" Nellie throws herself against me

and Jenny and Bridget. Aunt Cornelia is right behind her, tightly holding William's hand. All three of them look pale and tired. Their clothing is wrinkled, and William holds a rough gray blanket around his shoulders. But they're here, safe and sound.

I kneel down and take William's hand. "Are you hungry?" I ask him gently. I look up at Nellie. Her eyes sparkle with tears but her smile is the warm, gentle smile I've always known.

William nods. There are circles under his eyes. "Can we go home?" His voice is so little. I squeeze his hand in mine and then stand and hug him close against my side. I wrap my other arm around Nellie. I'm never going to let them go—ever.

A few days later, I step out onto the street with Bridget and Jenny. There is something important we want to do. We have been so very lucky—our family is safe. But many, many families have not been so fortunate. Relief funds have been set up for the hundreds of widows and orphans. Many are very poor now that they've lost their husbands and fathers who provided for them.

The offices of the *Titanic* Relief Fund are only a few blocks away, and we're going to find a way to help. Sorting the food donations, counting and recording the money donations—I know there's something we can do.

Here it is—300 Fourth Avenue, just like the newspaper said. A big white sign in the window reads TITANIC RELIEF FUND OFFICES—INQUIRE WITHIN. I push open the glass-and-oak door. Inside, a young woman sits at a desk, writing. She looks up.

"I'm Samantha Parkington," I say as I approach the desk. "These are my sisters. We're here to help."

Epilogue

Titanic lay silent on the seabed for more than seventy years. The wreck was so deep that the water pressure would crush any divers who tried to reach it. In addition, for years no one knew *exactly* where *Titanic* had come to rest.

In 1985, an underwater robot called Argo descended to the ocean floor, 12,000 feet down. Argo was controlled by a French-American team, led by Robert Ballard, in a ship above. Argo found *Titanic* resting in two pieces on the ocean floor, one-third of a mile apart. The front piece, the bow, was mostly intact. Some of the light fixtures still hung from the ceiling. The stern, the back part that bobbed in the water and sank last, was a twisted wreck. In between the two pieces lay scattered wreckage: wine bottles, pieces of coal, dolls, bedsprings, leather shoes.

Rusted bow of *Titanic*, found in the North Atlantic Ocean

The bodies of the people who had sunk with the ship had long ago been consumed by ocean life. Marine **organisms** were slowly eating away at the metal of the ship as well. Pictures were taken, and the wreck was studied and mapped. Artifacts such as dishes, buttons, lamps, and eyeglasses were brought to the surface. But the ship itself can never be raised. The material is far too delicate to survive a journey to the surface. *Titanic* will remain as scraps of rust and metal on the sea floor.

Glossary

Bow – the front of a ship

Bowels – the interior parts of a ship

Capsize – when a boat turns over in the water

Dry dock – a vessel that can be flooded and drained of water, to be used for the construction or repair of ships

Emigrate – to leave your own country in order to live in another one

Gangplank – a short bridge or piece of wood used for walking onto and off of a ship

Gantry – a frame consisting of scaffolds

Hull – the frame or body of a boat or ship

Hypothermic – having a dangerously low body temperature

Immigrant – someone who comes from abroad to live permanently in a country

Inquiry – a study or investigation

Laborer – someone employed to do physical work

Morse code – a way of signaling that uses light or sound in a pattern of dots and dashes to represent letters

Organism – a living plant or animal

Prejudice – an unfair opinion about someone based on their race, religion, or other characteristic

Quartermaster – an officer on a ship in charge of signals or navigation

Steerage – accommodations in the lowest level of a ship near the steering machinery

Stern – the back of a ship

Steward – an employee on a ship who assists passengers

Telegraph – a device for sending messages over long distances

Tuberculosis – a highly contagious bacterial disease that usually affects the lungs

Source Notes

Adler, Susan A., and Maxine Rose Schur. *Manners and Mischief: A Samantha Classic, Vol. 1.* Middleton, WI: American Girl Publishing, 1986.

"British Wreck Commissioner's Inquiry, Day 3: Testimony of Frederick Barrett." *Titanic Inquiry Project.* http://www.titanicinquiry.org /BOTInq/BOTInq03Barrett01.php.

Buckey, Sarah Masters. *The Stolen Sapphire: A Samantha Mystery.* Middleton, WI: American Girl Publishing, 2006.

Carson, Rob. "Someone Wins, Someone Loses In Tale of Ticket." *The News Tribune.* Tacoma, WA. http://faculty.law.lsu.edu/ccorcos/lawctr /titanicstory.htm.

"Colonel Archibald Gracie IV." *Encyclopedia Titanica: 1st Class Passengers.* https://www.encyclopedia-titanica.org/titanic-survivor/colonel -archibald-gracie.html.

Eaton, John P., and Charles A. Haas. *Titanic: Destination Disaster: The Legends and the Reality.* New York: W.W. Norton & Co, 1987.

Gregson, Sarah. "Women and Children First? The Administration of *Titanic* Relief in Southampton, 1912–59." *English Historical Review.* Volume CXXVII, Issue 524, pp. 83–109.

Kiger, Patrick J. "Life on Board: Recreation: Games and Activities Available to the Passengers of *Titanic.*" *National Geographic: Titanic 100 Years.* http://channel.nationalgeographic.com/titanic-100-years/articles /life-on-board-recreation/.

King, Carol, and Richard Havers. *Titanic: The Unfolding Story.* Somerset, UK: Haynes Publishing, 2011.

Lynch, Don. *Titanic: An Illustrated History.* New York: Hyperion, 1992.

"Miss Eva Miriam Hart." *Encyclopedia Titanica: 2nd Class Passengers.* https://www.encyclopedia-titanica.org/titanic-survivor/eva-hart .html.

"Mrs. Charlotte Caroline Collyer (nee Tate)." *Encyclopedia Titanica: 2nd Class Passengers.* www.encyclopedia-titanica.org/titanic-survivor /charlotte-annie-collyer.html#pictures.

Raymer, Dottie. *Samantha's Ocean Liner Adventure.* Middleton, WI: Pleasant Company Publications, 2002.

Scarrott, Joseph. "An Account of the *Titanic* Disaster by a Survivor: The Sphere." *Encyclopedia Titanica.* https://www.encyclopedia-titanica .org/an-account-of-the-titanic-disaster-by-a-survivor.html.

Titanic: The Tragedy That Shook the World, One Century Later. New York: Life Books, 2012.

"Titanic's Boilers." *Titanic-Titanic.com.* http://www.titanic-titanic.com /titanic_boilers.shtml.

Tripp, Valerie. *Lost and Found: A Samantha Classic, Vol. 2.* Middleton, WI: American Girl Publishing, 1987.

Wels, Susan. *Titanic: Legacy of the World's Greatest Ocean Liner.* San Diego, CA: Tehabi Books, 1997.

Welshman, John. *Titanic: The Last Night of a Small Town.* Oxford, UK: Oxford University Press, 2012.

Young, Filson. *Titanic: The Original Book About the Catastrophe Published Only 37 Days After Its Sinking.* 1912. Reprint. North Charleston, SC: CreateSpace Independent Publishing Platform, 2014.

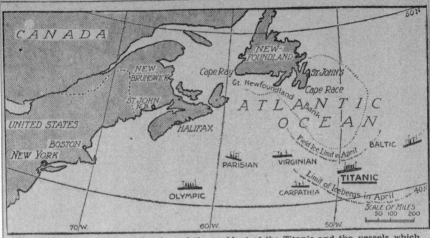

Approximate positions at the time of the accident of the Titanic and the vessels which went to her assistance.

100

Timeline

1908 – Construction of *Olympic* begins in December

1909 – Construction of *Titanic* begins in March

1911 – *Olympic* collides with another ship; *Titanic*'s maiden voyage delayed

1912, April 2 – *Titanic* leaves Belfast, Ireland, for overnight voyage to Southampton, England

1912, April 10

> **7:30 a.m.** – Captain Smith boards *Titanic* with a full crew for her maiden voyage

> **9:30-11:30 a.m.** – Second- and third-class passengers board the ship

> **11:30 a.m.** – First-class passengers board and are escorted to their cabins

> **12:00 p.m.** – *Titanic* leaves Southampton

1912, April 14

9:00 a.m. – Senior Operator Jack Phillips receives first message of the day warning of icebergs ahead

10:15 a.m. – Captain Smith is given his first iceberg warning

12:00 p.m. – Phillips receives a second iceberg warning from the ship *Baltic*

5:50 p.m. – Captain Smith makes the decision to change *Titanic*'s course

9:40 p.m. – Phillips receives fifth iceberg warning from the ship *Mesaba*, but doesn't deliver it to the bridge or Captain Smith

10:00 p.m. – First Officer Murdoch takes over on the bridge

11:00 p.m. – *Californian* sends message to *Titanic* saying she has stopped for the night due to ice

11:39 p.m. – Lookout Frederick Fleet spots an iceberg

11:40 p.m. – Murdoch orders the engine room to stop; *Titanic* strikes an iceberg

1912, April 15

12:00 a.m. – Captain Smith orders a distress call for help

12:20 a.m. – Order given to start loading lifeboats with women and children

2:18 a.m. – *Titanic*'s lights go out and the ship breaks in two halves; the bow sinks

2:20 a.m. – The stern floats for a few minutes, then begins to sink

4:10 a.m. – The first lifeboat is picked up by *Carpathia*

1912, April 18 – *Carpathia* arrives in New York

1985 – An expedition led by Robert Ballard discovers the wreck site of *Titanic* on the floor of the Atlantic Ocean using an underwater robot named Argo